Children who want to know where the tremendous power comes from that is needed to drive airliners along at 2,000 miles an hour, or to hurl rockets into space at 25,000 miles an hour, are also likely to wonder not only how the engines in these machines work, but also how and why engines came to be invented at all.

This book provides an easily understood outline showing how, as man became more civilized, he had a greater and greater need for engines to help him grow food in bigger quantities, to make life possible in difficult climates and make more of the good things of life available to more people. Perhaps the most outstanding effect of the development of engines has been the development of cheaper and easier means of travel over longer distances. Man can now not only visit his neighbors, but he can in a short space of time visit people and get to know them in their homes in the farthest corners of the earth.

Starting with the primitive steam engine, Paul Roberson explains why and when it was first built, and shows how engineers proceeded to develop new kinds of engine that would produce more power for a lower consumption of fuel. The big changes in power needed for generating electricity cheaply in the huge quantities needed by civilized man and for getting man out into space, are explained in simple text that serves to amplify the clear and attractive illustrations.

The book concludes with a simple explanation of some of the new words that have to be introduced in a text dealing with the most modern technology.

Finding Out About SCIENCE

Edited by
KURT ROWLAND

ENGINES

By PAUL ROBERSON

Illustrated by TOM SWIMMER
and LASZLO ACS

Golden Press • New York

THIS EDITION PUBLISHED 1966 BY GOLDEN PRESS, INC., NEW YORK.

Copyright © 1965 by The John Day Company Inc. and Weidenfeld & Nicolson (Educational) Ltd. All rights reserved. This book, or parts thereof, must not be reproduced in any form without permission. This edition printed in the U.S.A. by Western Printing and Lithographing Company.

Contents

Man, power and engines 6
The steam engine 9
The steam turbine 17
The internal combustion engine 20
The gas turbine 28
About movement 32
The jet engine 36
The rocket 42
Efficiency 44
Communications 46

A long time ago men did not live in cities; they wandered from place to place and lived on whatever plants and animals they could find. But in time these primitive people settled down in one place and learned to till the soil; they became farmers. They used their animals to lighten the heavy work which goes with farming, such as plowing and threshing, invented simple "engines" such as levers and pulleys to make the most of the available muscle power. But man's need for more power drove him to look for other sources of power.

Perhaps the work of floods, thunderstorms and gales made him realize that nature abounds in energy on an enormous scale. So he invented devices such as watermills and windmills which would capture some of this natural energy and set it to do useful work.

But even though the *elements* were more powerful than the muscles of his animals, they still did not satisfy all his needs, for they were, on the whole, unreliable. Many attempts were made to invent "perpetual motion" machines that would work forever without needing outside help from wind or water. It was not until much later, when men knew more about engines, that they understood the reasons why such machines were impossible.

This "perpetual motion" machine could not actually work—the weights on each side are equal

During the 18th century water power was still used to drive the machines of the first factories to be built, such as those which spun yarn and wove cloth.

In Lancashire, England, where the warm, wet climate was just right for working with cotton, people also found many fast streams running down through lovely valleys. The factories were built where the power was, the valleys were spoiled and men changed from being farm hands to creatures shut up in dirty, noisy factories for long hours every day. Gradually, because wind and water power tended to be fitful and because it was difficult to get more than a certain amount of power from a river, factory owners turned to the new power, steam, based on the coal dug from the ground below their factories. In most places where coal was found, like the Pittsburgh area in Pennsylvania, the West Riding of Yorkshire, and the Ruhr valley in Germany, industries expanded or were set up.

Steam engines used steam made by burning coal to boil water. These engines could work harder than a horse because they "ate" more "food" more quickly. The food of the steam engine is coal which is burned up to give heat just as a man "burns" bread and meat to produce his energy and a horse "burns" hay or grass.

The first real job the steam engine was called upon to do was to pump water from the coal mines. To meet growing demand, miners had dug deeper into the ground and had met underground rivers that they could not drain with their normal treadmill or bucket pumps.

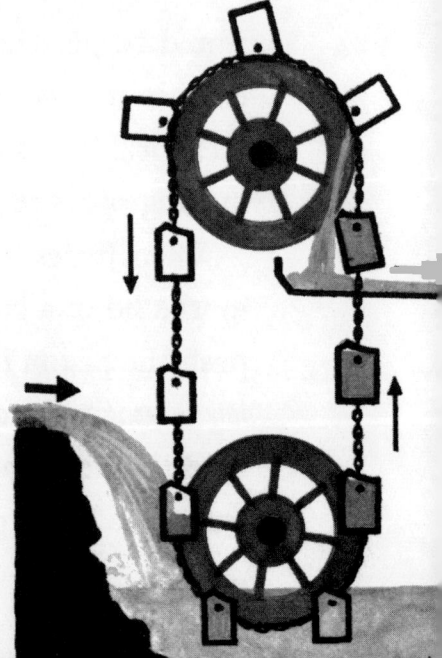

An early scheme, waterfall driven, for raising water for agriculture

When steam is cooled down it turns into water; this process is called *condensation*. But the volume of water so obtained is smaller than the volume of steam from which it comes. If you fill a tin can with steam and turn the steam into water by cooling it, the space above the water is almost a *vacuum* (a space where there is no air or any other gas). In the steam-filled can the steam pressure inside balances the air pressure outside. But a can containing a near-vacuum cannot resist the pressure of the air outside, and so the can collapses. If this can were fitted with a movable wall, this wall

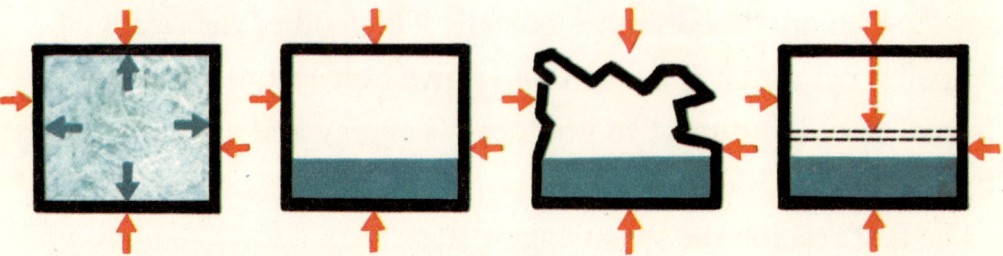

would be pushed in and this is exactly how the early steam engines worked. As you can see, it was the air which did all the work. The steam container is called the *cylinder* and the moving part the *piston*.

When James Watt (1736-1819) saw how steam could push up the lid of a kettle he had the idea of making the steam push the piston in and out. His steam engine had a balanced *horizontal* beam coupled on one side to the piston and on the other to the pump shaft. As the piston was pushed down, the pump shaft was pulled up and water forced up to the surface.

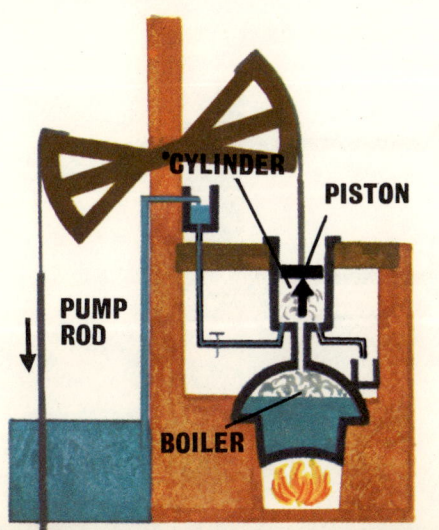

Left: The pump-rod weight raises the piston and sucks steam into the cylinder

Right: A cold water spray condenses the steam and creates a vacuum beneath the piston. Air pressure pushes it down and so raises the pump rod

These engines were improved by Watt and his partner, Boulton, who got rid of the water spray (shown in the diagram on page 11) and made the engine do four times as much work as the older types for the same amount of coal. They applied them to pumping, to grinding corn, to spinning cotton and to working metal including *forging* iron.

Watt's idea was further improved by the Cornishman Trevithick who introduced the *double acting* engine in 1800. It is still used today in steam locomotives.

With the slide valve in the position shown, steam passes into the cylinder behind the piston and pushes it from right to left. The crank is turned and moves the valve to the position shown below.

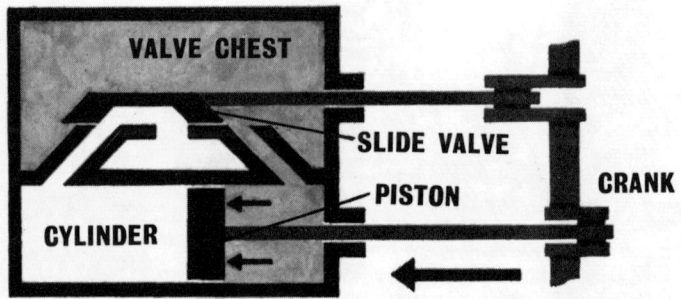

Steam now enters the cylinder on the left and pushes the piston from left to right, continuing to rotate the crank. Exhausted steam is driven out by the piston through a port (not shown)

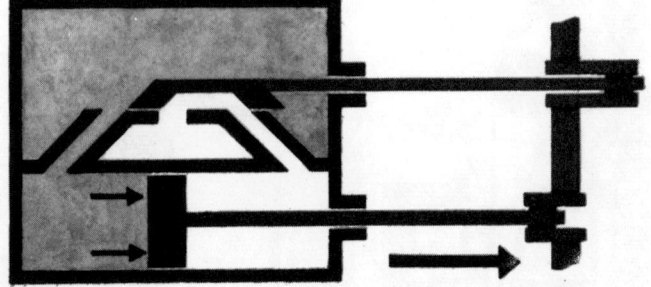

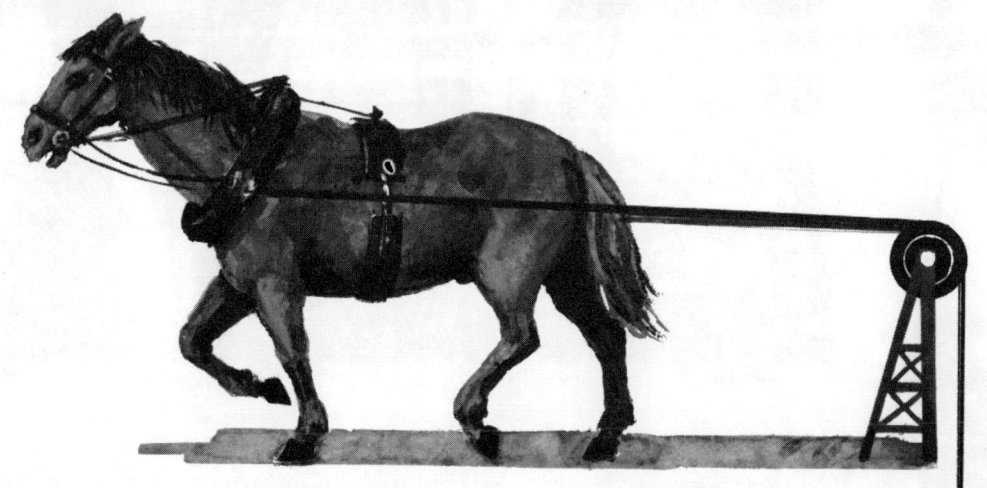

When engines began to be used everywhere, engineers found they had to be able to say how strong an engine needed to be to do a given job, or how much work it could do in a given time. Watt measured how hard a horse could work. He found that by pulling a rope running over a pulley, a horse could raise a 150-pound basket of coal 220 feet up a mine shaft in a minute. This, he said, is the same as raising 550 pounds through one foot in one second, and this speed of doing work he called one *horse power*, h.p. for short. A big modern machine could lift 55 million pounds of coal up through one foot in a second; it can work a hundred thousand times as hard as a horse and it can do it day after day and month after month without stopping or getting tired.

In a factory such as a cotton mill, the steam engine with its boiler would be placed in the basement or on the ground floor so that it was easy to feed in the fuel—coal. The engine itself would drive a big flywheel which by its weight would tend to keep things running smoothly. The drive would be taken up from floor to floor by endless leather belts, each driving the pulley on a long shaft from which each loom or spinning machine would be driven by other belts. This system could be used for driving any other kind of machines.

The steam engine was set to drive ships around the beginning of the 19th century and finally took the place of sails, again because the power supply could be relied upon to get the ship to its port more quickly and on time. In the first ships the engines drove paddlewheels, but later screw propellers were shown to waste less of the power provided by the engine and they took the place of paddles except in boats running in shallow water. To make use of the heat of the fuel, the steam in ships' engines was used in one cylinder after another before returning to the boiler as water. But even so not more than one-sixth of the fuel's heat was used. The steam engine was also used to drive *traction engines* on the road and to power railway *locomotives*.

In the new age of industry the steam engine really came into its own for moving goods and people cheaply and quickly and to drive the electrical generators which started to come into use toward the end of the 19th century, following the discoveries of Michael Faraday (1791-1867). For all these uses, the up-and-down movement of the piston had to be turned into a round-and-round movement to turn wheels for moving

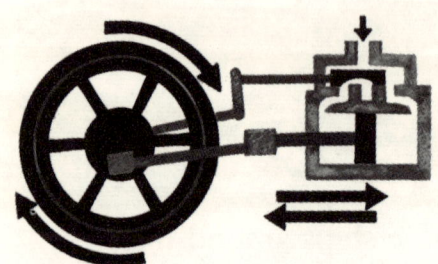

The sort of double-acting steam engine used to drive early dynamos to generate electricity

trains, to turn paddle wheels or propellers for driving ships or for turning shafts in mills or generators in power stations. The up-and-down movement was a nuisance and so was the fact that the steam had to be made in a separate part of the plant, the boiler. Not only were these boilers very big and heavy, but they were expensive and caused a certain amount of wastage of fuel. For this reason, men began to look for an engine which would give a rotary (round-and-round) movement from the outset and which would also have a smaller appetite for fuel.

Heron's "water sprinkler" type of steam turbine in use 150 B.C.

The first step forward came when Charles Parsons (1854-1931) looked into an idea used by the Greek, Heron. In the year 150 B.C. Heron had made a steam *turbine* by passing steam into a ball, arranged so that it could turn around while letting the steam escape through two pipes, one on each side of the ball and each bent over in opposite directions, rather like a lawn sprinkler. This device would spin around at high speed and Parsons' model worked quite well, but he could see the difficulties of manufacture. He therefore switched over to another idea for making a gas turn a wheel around. This was the early form of turbine in which sails are blown around by the wind, rather like a windmill. Parsons found that the

17th Century idea for steam turbine

Steam turbine "windmills" have many more "sails" than an ordinary windmill and, for efficiency, each one is shaped like an airplane wing. This principle is employed in large industrial turbine installations, such as the one shown on the opposite page

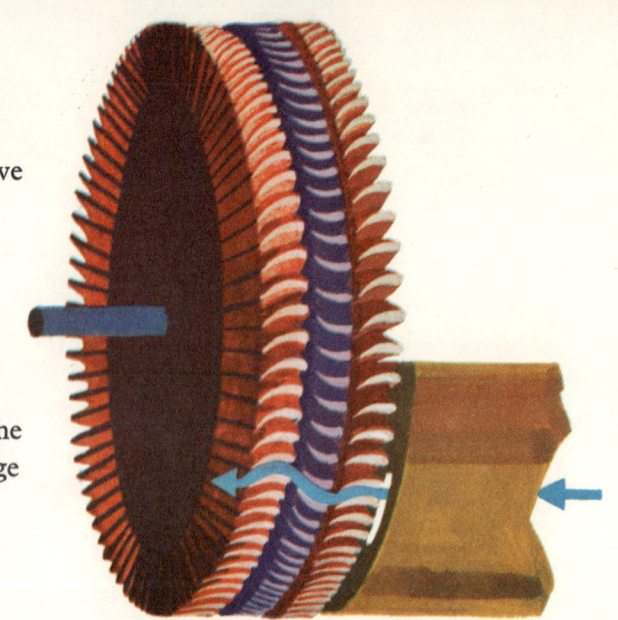

system could be made to operate if only a little work was expected from each of a number of separate "windmills," one following another, the steam being re-directed by fixed "sails" between each two "windmills."

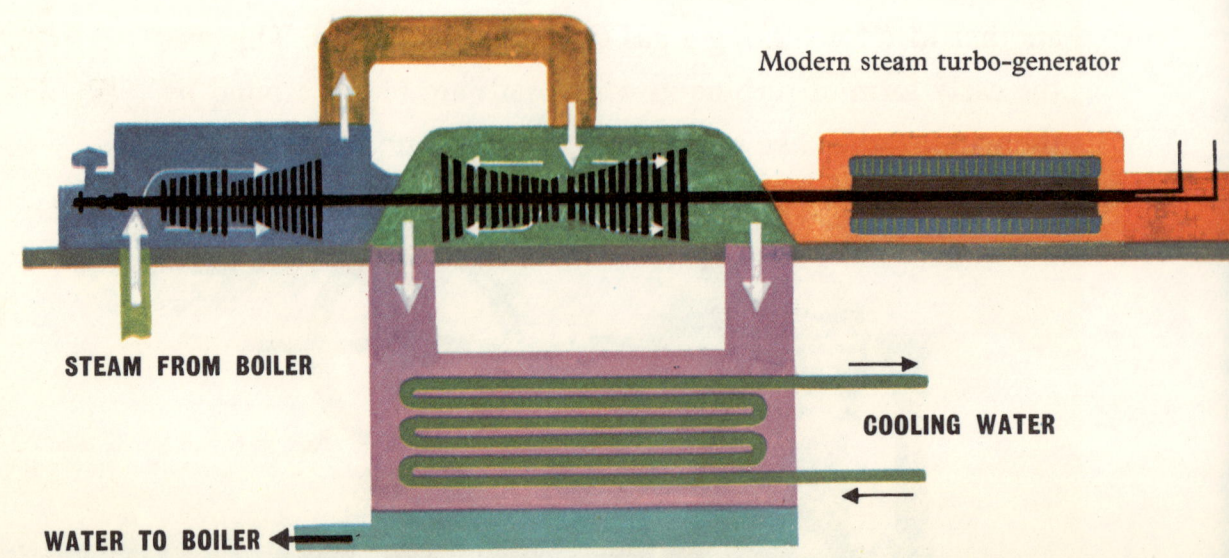

Modern steam turbo-generator

STEAM FROM BOILER

COOLING WATER

WATER TO BOILER

This idea quickly caught on and proved successful not only because it was smooth and free from shaking but also because a large amount of power was produced by a very small machine. The machine proved able to convert much more of the heat of the fuel into useful work and above all it produced a turning movement directly and did not require any *cranks*.

Parsons' steam turbine was developed into powerful engines for driving power station *generators*, and big ones today can do the work of several hundred thousand horses and turn into useful work nearly two-fifths of the heat of the fuel that is burned to supply them with steam. They are also used to power the big passenger-carrying liners that plow through the seas at speeds up to forty miles an hour, and for factories where steam is used in the preparation of foodstuffs such as sugar.

Steam turbines, good as they are, still suffer from the disadvantage of having their steam made in a separate place, in a boiler. This means that heat is wasted and that more fuel is burned than needs to be.

The first successful engines which worked without a separate boiler used coal gas as fuel by mixing it with air drawn into the cylinder of something like a steam engine, making it burn and using the expanding gas to push down the piston. But real success came with the development of the *internal combustion engine* by Otto, Daimler, Siemens, Diesel and others. In the ordinary internal combustion engine a mixture of air and fuel is drawn into the *combustion chamber*, compressed and exploded by an electric spark. In the Diesel engine air only is drawn into the combustion chamber and compressed so much that it gets very hot. When diesel oil is sprayed into it, the oil spray explodes without the help of a spark.

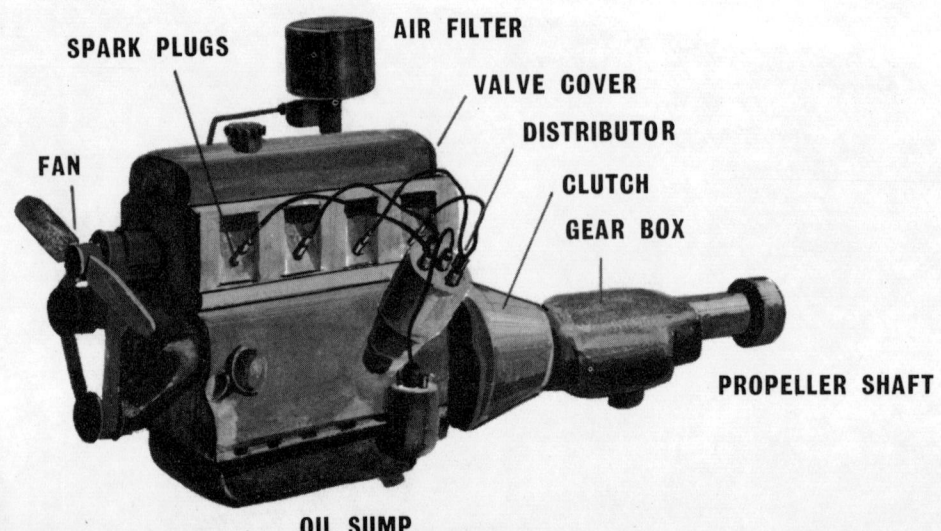

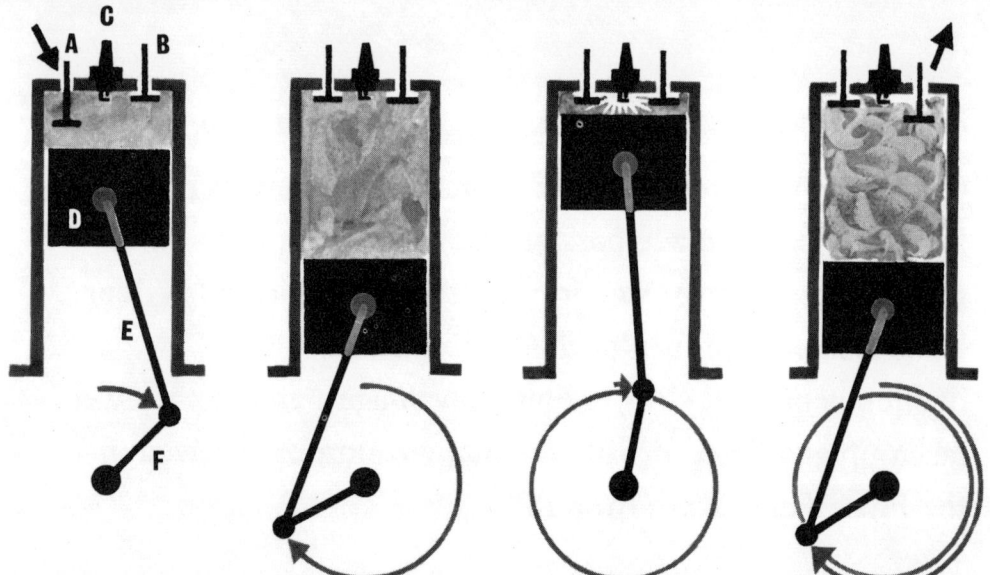

Above: Four stroke car engine
First stroke (down) piston D sucks in gasoline/air mixture through inlet valve A. Second stroke (up) mixture is compressed and fired by spark plug C. Third stroke (down) burning gas drives piston turning crank F through connecting rod E. Fourth stroke (up) piston pushes out burnt exhaust gas B

Below: (*left*) Two stroke engine has no valves. Gasoline/air mixture compressed in crankcase by descending piston driven down by burning gas. Fresh mixture sweeps out exhaust as ports uncover.

Below: (*right*) Diesel engine has no spark plug. Fuel/air mixture lights itself by heat of compression

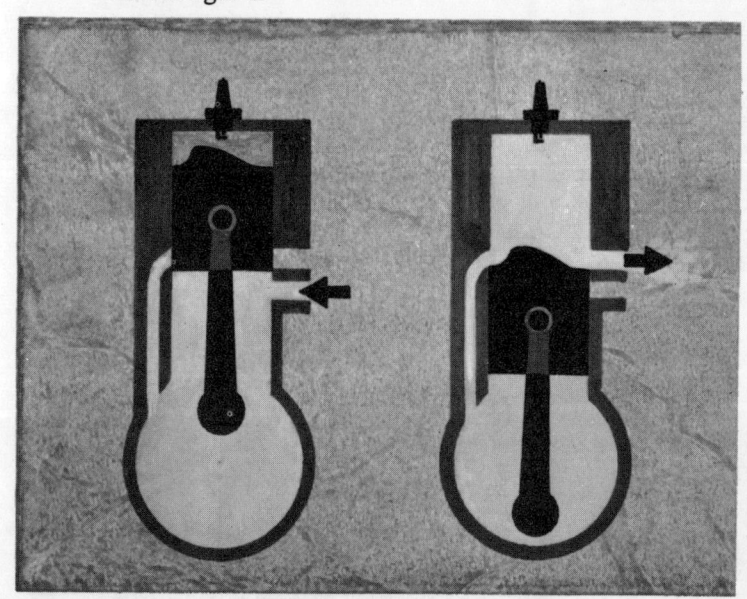

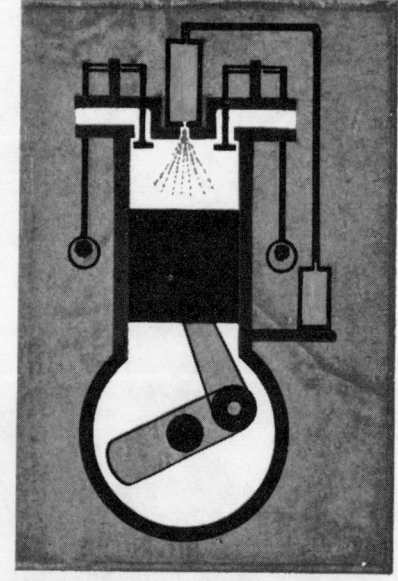

Internal combustion engines were put to use in the horseless carriage or automobile. Their promise of high power and light weight also made possible the production of the first real airplane by two American brothers, Orville and Wilbur Wright, about the turn of the century. Both these developments had clear military advantages, and so they were taken up and developed by the many countries involved in the First World War (1914-18).

The early cars were really horseless carriages; they were heavy and slow with slow moving engines that did not produce much power for their size and weight, while their bodies looked like the horse-drawn carriages from which they had sprung.

Fairly widespread use of motor vehicles in the First World War led to progress in car and truck design and reliability. The new machines were designed as motor vehicles right from the start.

The advances that led to the production of the modern car and its high efficiency engine were the work of a few men who could see into the future and who believed that the motor car had big possibilities. Outstanding among these men was Henry Ford (1863-1947) who invented the method of making cheap, reliable cars by the million so that every man could afford to drive one. Herbert Austin produced the world's first successful baby car, the famous Austin 7, in 1922. This started the process of getting lots of power from a

small engine, and the development of racing engines also helped in the new trend. Some of these engines give about 200 h.p. from a capacity of only 1½ liters, and many of the features which had to be thought out in order to make them so efficient can now be found in the ordinary engines of family cars.

The work of these pioneers changed the popular motor car from a handbuilt horseless carriage costing more than twice the annual wages of a skilled workman in 1913 to a machine that is better than the most costly car of those days and which today costs less than one-third of the annual wages of a skilled workman.

By the end of the First World War, reliable aircraft engines of about 100 h.p. were commonplace. These could drive small airplanes through the skies at about 100 miles an hour—the speed at which the dogfights took place above the battlefields of Flanders. Even then it was realized that more speed would be an advantage and the designers always tried to get a little more power for the pilot. When scientists learned more about airplanes, they realized that to double the speed of an airplane from 100 to 200 m.p.h. they needed an engine giving not twice the horse power but four times as much, or 400 h.p. Similarly for 300 m.p.h. one would need 900 h.p. and for 400 m.p.h., 1600 h.p.

To double the speed of an airplane, roughly four times as much power is needed from the engine. For an increase of three times, an engine nine times as powerful must be used

To enable airplanes to fly faster and to carry more useful loads, engines were needed which could produce more power without being any heavier. This was done by producing better and lighter metals from which the engine parts could be made, by using bigger and bigger cylinders and pistons and then, when no more power could be obtained by making the cylinder bigger, using more and more cylinders in a single engine. Famous engines such as the Rolls-Royce *Eagle* and the Wright Cyclone were finally able to deliver about 3500 h.p. and both had very large *capacities* (that is, the combined volume of all their cylinders) of 50 to 100 liters. The big *radial engines* like the Wright Cyclone finally had 18 cylinders in two rows and could produce their power for a very small relative consumption of gasoline. These engines were the basis on which world-wide airlines were built up.

Nearly forty years ago, farsighted engineers realized that if airplanes were to go really fast or to carry big loads, a new type of engine would be needed, one that would be lighter, smaller and *much* more powerful than anything possible from the development of piston engines. This meant a turbine, the kind of engine known to give high power from small frames, which would use hot gas not made in outside heaters or boilers but inside the engine itself. Such an engine, a *gas turbine*, would be the last word and would have every advantage that an "earthbound" engine should have—no vibration and no cranks because it would develop its power from rotating parts, and no boiler because it would produce its heat inside the engine.

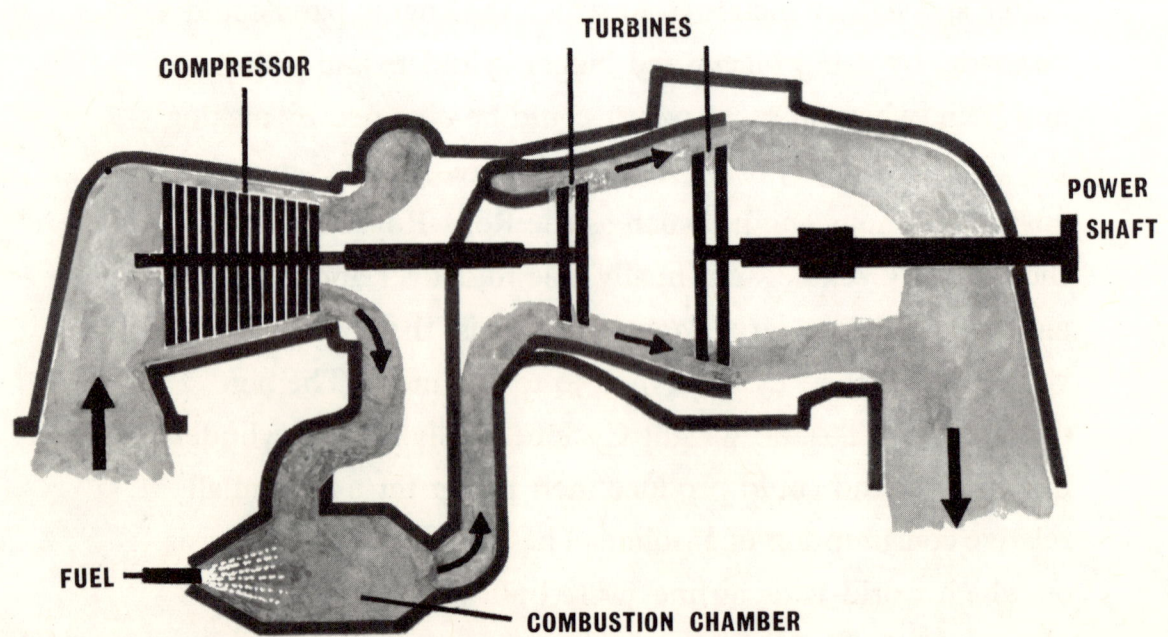

A centrifugal compressor

A simple combustion chamber

A simple turbine wheel

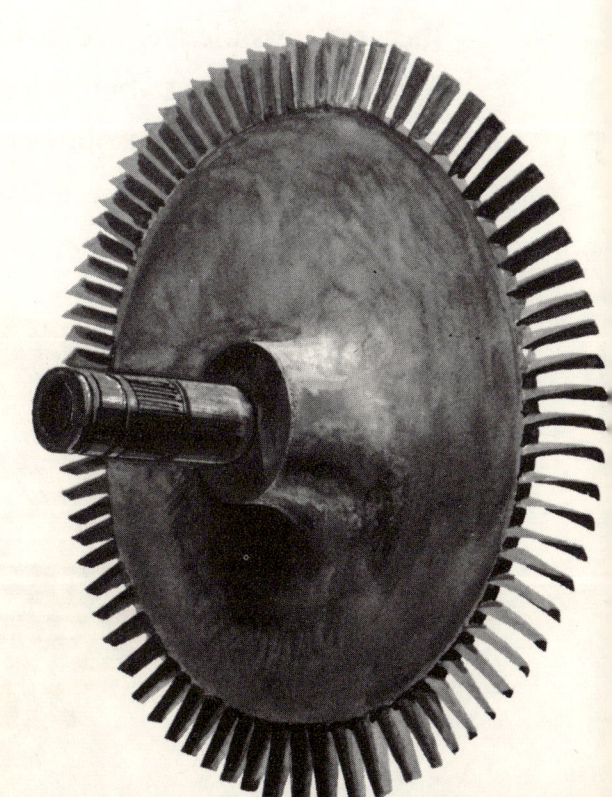

The three main parts of a gas turbine are—compressor, combustion chamber, turbine. The first draws air into the engine and raises it to high pressure. In the second, fuel is burnt in the air which is heated to a high temperature. The third extracts work from the hot air and uses it to drive the compressor and other machines. Sometimes a heat exchanger is used to recover waste heat from the turbine exhaust and return it to air leaving the compressor

Gas turbines have been used to drive locomotives, ships and motor cars. In ships the gas turbine can be used to drive an electric generator which supplies power to electric motors to drive the ship; it can also be used to drive the propeller directly. It is this second kind that is used in fast naval patrol boats, destroyers and frigates to help them reach high speeds and to get out of harbor quickly while steam is being raised for the main engines. Until recently gas turbines could not be used for driving cars because they allowed too much heat to escape through the exhaust, so that too much fuel had to be used. But with good *heat exchangers* fitted, which re-use some of this heat, as you can see in the picture, such cars have become possible and are now being made. They can achieve over 100 m.p.h. at about 18 miles a gallon, no more than ordinary cars with gasoline engines of the same power. *But* the gas turbine engine should last for half a million miles— enough to outlast three or four bodies.

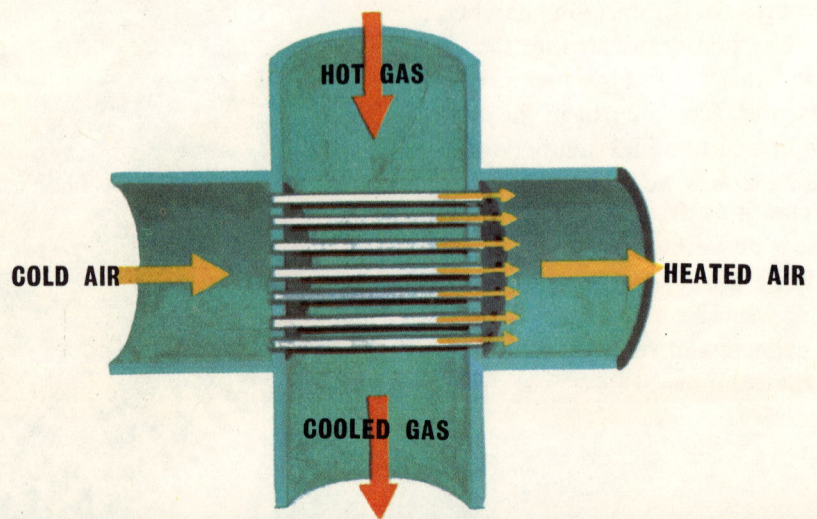

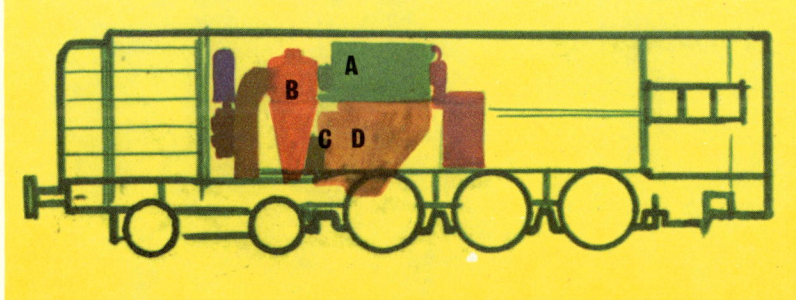

Left: The world's first direct-drive gas turbine railway engine produces 2,700 HP for hauling expresses at 90 MPH.

A — Heat exchanger

B — Combustion chamber

C — Compressor

D — Turbine

Below: The engine space of the latest Rover gas turbine driven saloon car

A — Turbine exhaust

B — Heat exchangers

C — Compressor and combustion system

Before we discuss how such engines are applied to aircraft, let us consider how things move. On the ground practically all animals move themselves along by pushing against the ground. They pull on their muscles which move the limbs which push on the ground. In the water fishes move themselves about by pushing against the water. In the air, birds and animals have two jobs to do, to keep themselves up and to row themselves along by airplane wing action, which means pushing against the air.

Push is used in most machines for movement. In the case of the bicycle the leg pushes against the pedal which turns the wheel (through the chain) which pushes against the ground to drive the machine along. An engine can take the place of the muscle to drive the machine as in a motor bicycle or a car or a steam engine.

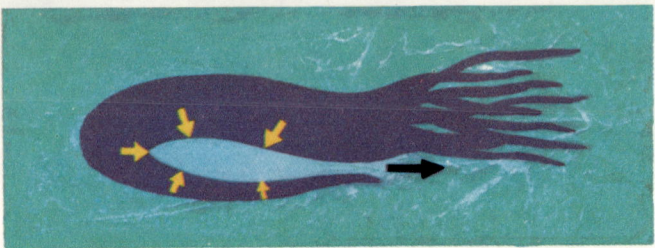

Some creatures move through the seas by a different kind of forward-driving force—*propulsion*. These are the squids and octopuses. These animals' bodies are large bags lined with strong muscles which can be filled with sea water. By pulling in its muscles the squid can tighten the bag and expel the water under pressure through a hole at one end. This drives the squid along by *jet propulsion*, which is really internal push, the push on the area inside the squid's bag that is opposite the hole at the back.

34

You can make a balloon shoot along by a form of jet propulsion similar to that used by the squid. All you have to do is to blow the balloon up and let it go without tying up the neck. The balloon will shoot all over the room propelled by the inside pressure on the little area opposite the neck.

All *rockets* move by this internal push. Solid fuel rockets contain a stick of material which will burn steadily but very quickly. This keeps up the pressure on the area inside the rocket opposite the hole and pushes the rocket along. Because the rocket is pushed along by internal push it will actually go better in a vacuum than in the air, because there is no air around to resist its progress.

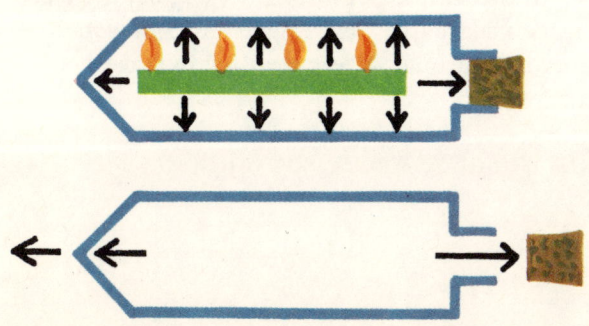

A rocket is pushed along by the pressure inside acting on the area opposite the jet hole

35

Gas turbines can be designed in which the turbine itself takes from the stream of fast-moving high-pressure gas only enough energy to drive the compressor. The pressure and heat energy which remain can be allowed to escape through a nozzle which stops the gas from rushing out so fast that the pressure is lost. Such an arrangement is called a *jet engine* and is used to drive aircraft by jet propulsion.

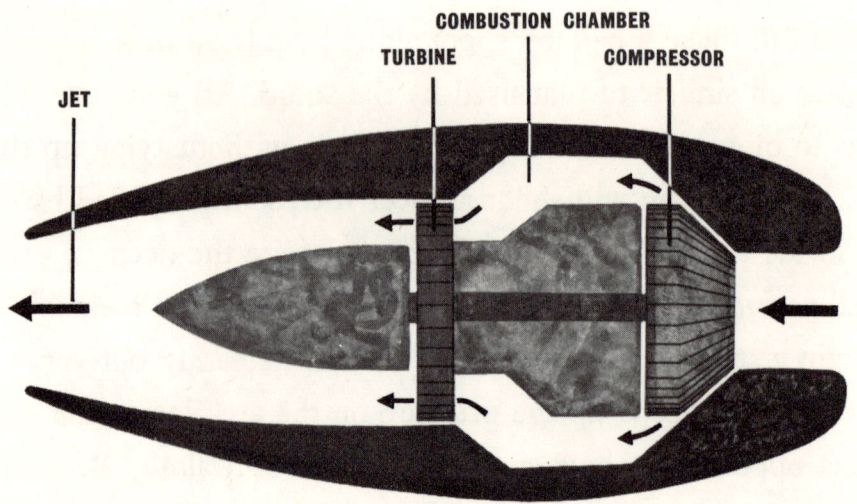

Above: In the simple gas turbine jet engine, there are only three main parts, the compressor, combustion chamber and turbine. These are used to make a propulsive jet

36

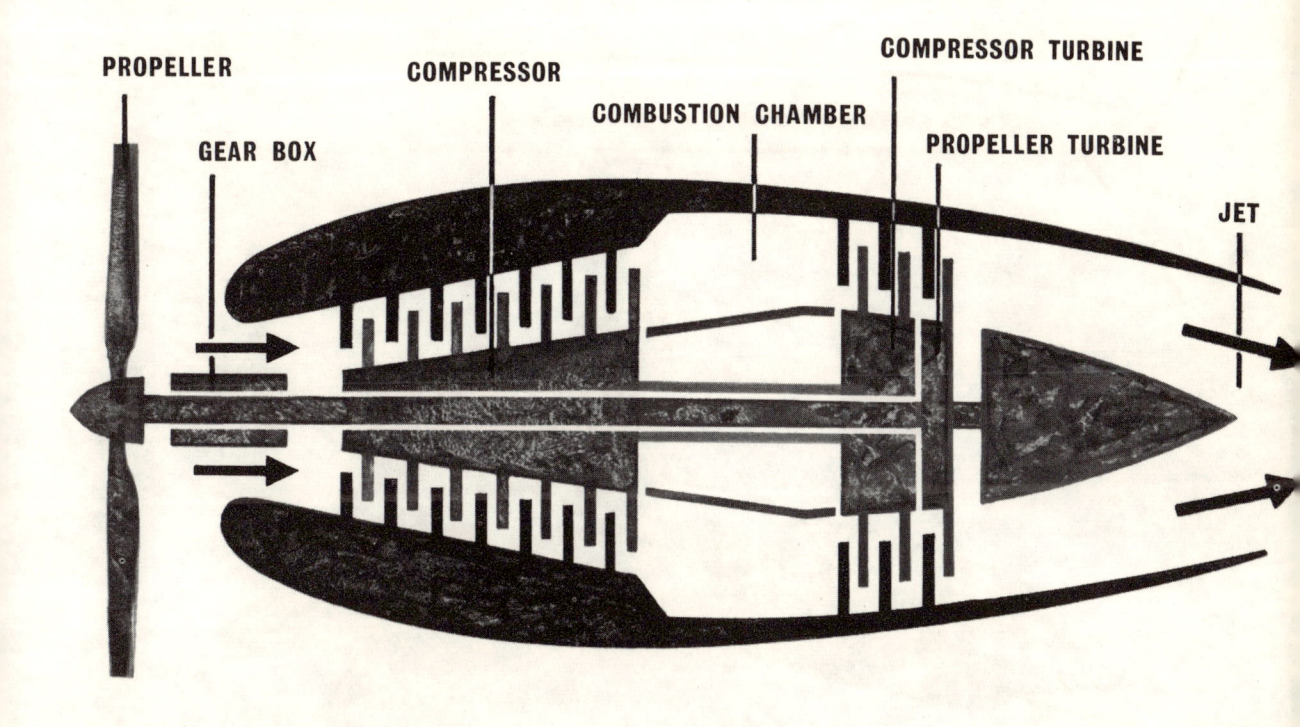

PROPELLER COMPRESSOR COMPRESSOR TURBINE
GEAR BOX COMBUSTION CHAMBER PROPELLER TURBINE
JET

Instead of allowing the gas to escape as a jet it can be made to turn a second turbine which drives a normal propeller. This is known as a *turbo-prop engine* and it is a very good engine for driving short range, low-speed airliners because it uses no more fuel than a piston engine. Turbo-prop engines can be very much more powerful than the biggest piston engines (engines of 10,000 h.p. have been made) and they have the advantage of being turbine-driven and are therefore much smoother.

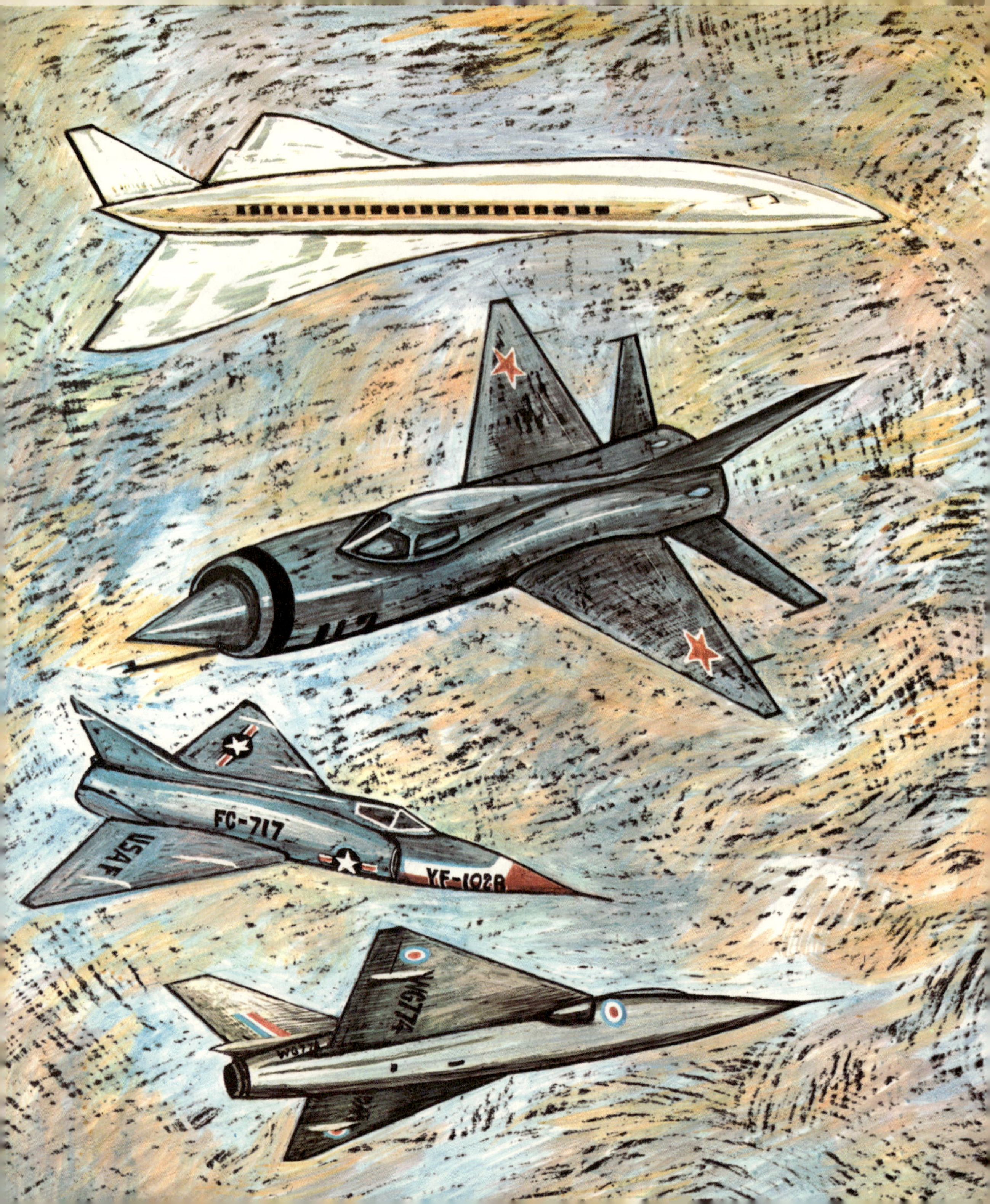
FC-717
USAF
YF-102B
WG774

The ram jet has no moving parts. It is best for driving aircraft at speeds above 2000 MPH

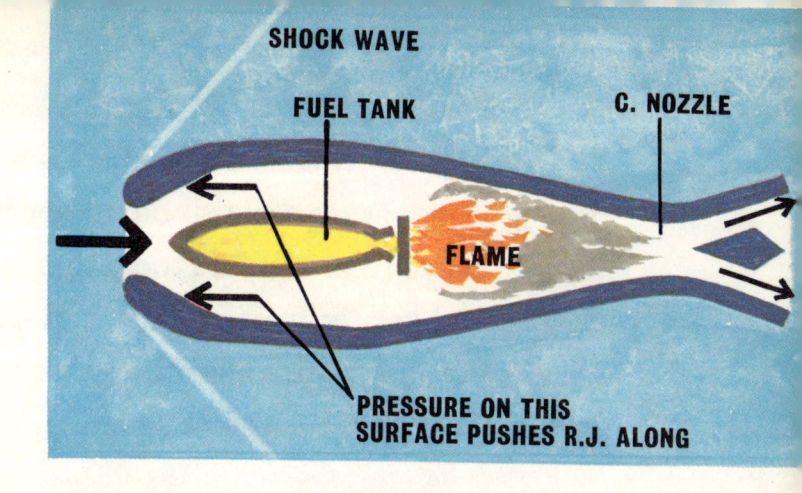

SHOCK WAVE
FUEL TANK
C. NOZZLE
FLAME
PRESSURE ON THIS SURFACE PUSHES R.J. ALONG

The *ram-jet* is an engine suitable for very high-speed flight at above 2000 m.p.h. At this speed it is the best kind of propulsion system. The ram-jet is a very simple engine with no basic moving parts. Air enters through the nose and is compressed by slowing down. It is then heated up, speeded up and exhausted through a *nozzle*. Ram-jets do not really begin to work well until they are moving at more than about 400 m.p.h., and can be used to drive the rotor of a *helicopter* which whirls around with its tips approaching *sonic speed*, that is, the speed of sound.

The very fast jet from an ordinary gas turbine is best for driving planes at high speed, but is not very good for getting them to move from rest. A type of gas turbine with a slower exhaust and greater masses of air, a *by-pass* engine, is better for this job and for driving planes that have to travel at speeds less than the speed of sound.

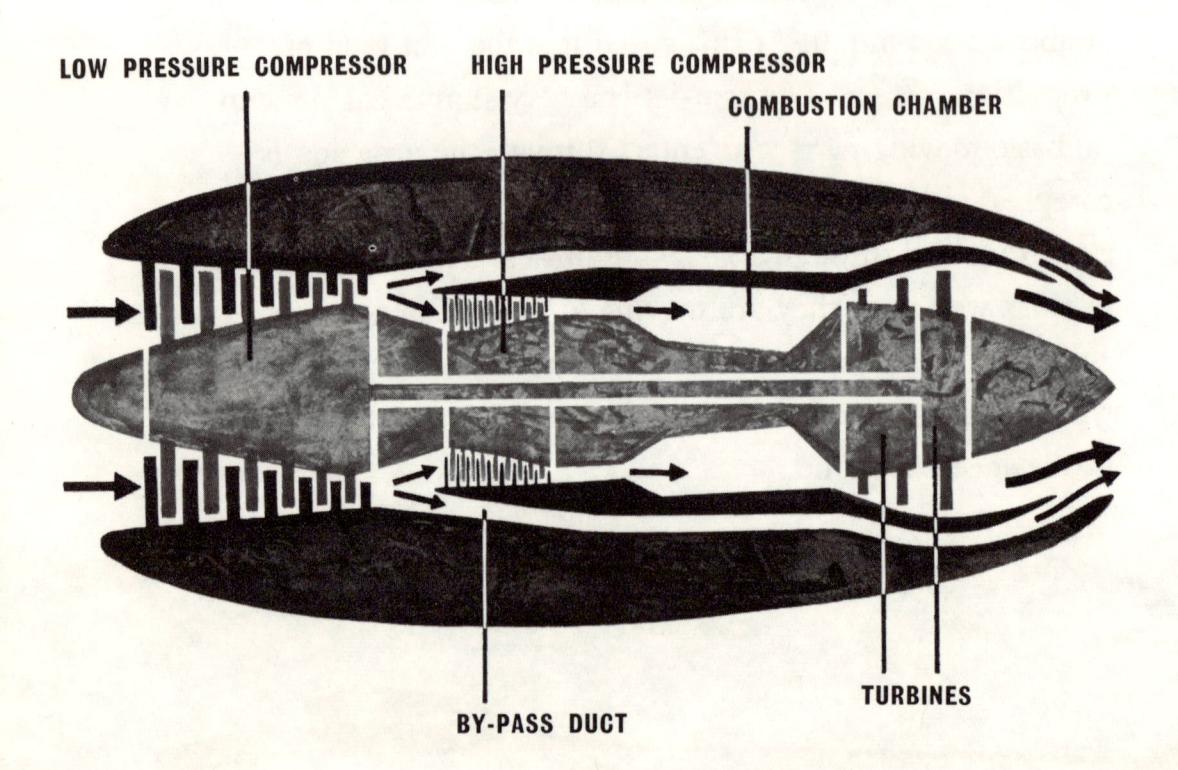

In the by-pass engine, only about half the air from the first compressor is further compressed and heated. The hot jet is surrounded by a cold one. Fuel consumption is low and the jet not so noisy

The modern by-pass jet engine can produce a push, or *thrust*, more than five times greater than its own weight. An engine weighing as little as 1000 pounds will produce more than 5000 pounds of thrust. If an airplane weighing 5000 pounds is fitted with an engine which can produce more than 5000 pounds of thrust, this thrust, if directed downward, will lift the airplane straight into the air. If the jet is now turned so that it points backward, the airplane will begin to move forward and go faster and faster until its wings can take over the job of keeping it up in the air. These airplanes are very exciting to watch and one can easily see that enormously long runways could quickly become a thing of the past.

KEROSENE

LIQUID OXYGEN

PUMPS

COMBUSTION CHAMBER

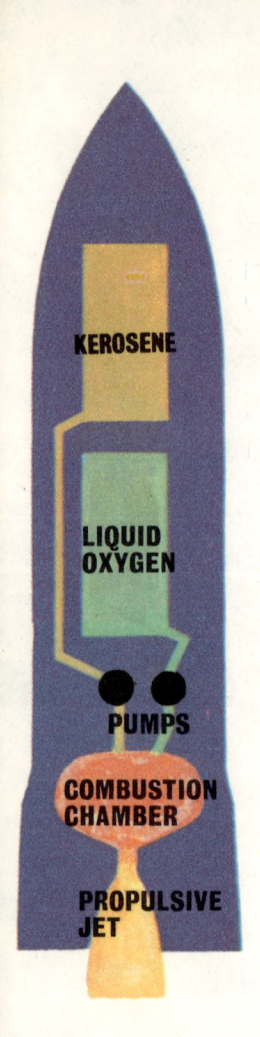

PROPULSIVE JET

The thrust of a jet engine comes from the air that passes through it. If such an engine is to work in space, where there is no air, it must eject a large amount of hot gas which it has to make from a fuel (such as kerosene) and something to burn with it—an *oxidant*. The fuel and the oxidant are carried separately and are only mixed in the combustion chamber.

42

To develop a thrust of 275,000 pounds, an average satellite booster rocket burns 26 tons of kerosene and 60 tons of liquid oxygen in the 180 seconds of its active life. These large loads of fuels which rockets have to carry when they start make it difficult to design one which can lift itself (and its fuel) right off the earth and into space. In fact, with ordinary fuels like kerosene and oxygen it cannot be done at all if only one rocket is used. In this case three rockets have to be fitted together to make what is called a three-stage rocket. The first one is the largest, which lifts itself and its smaller partners some 50 miles off the earth and reaches a speed of 8000 m.p.h. The second one then takes over, as the first stage drops away, and this boosts the speed to about 13,000 m.p.h. at about 80 miles up. Finally as the second stage burns out, the third rocket lights up and accelerates itself and its load to 18,000 m.p.h. In America the Saturn V booster rocket, which is intended for travel to the moon and beyond, will have five engines burning 4,500,000 pounds of kerosene and liquid oxygen in 150 seconds for 7,500,000 pounds of thrust.

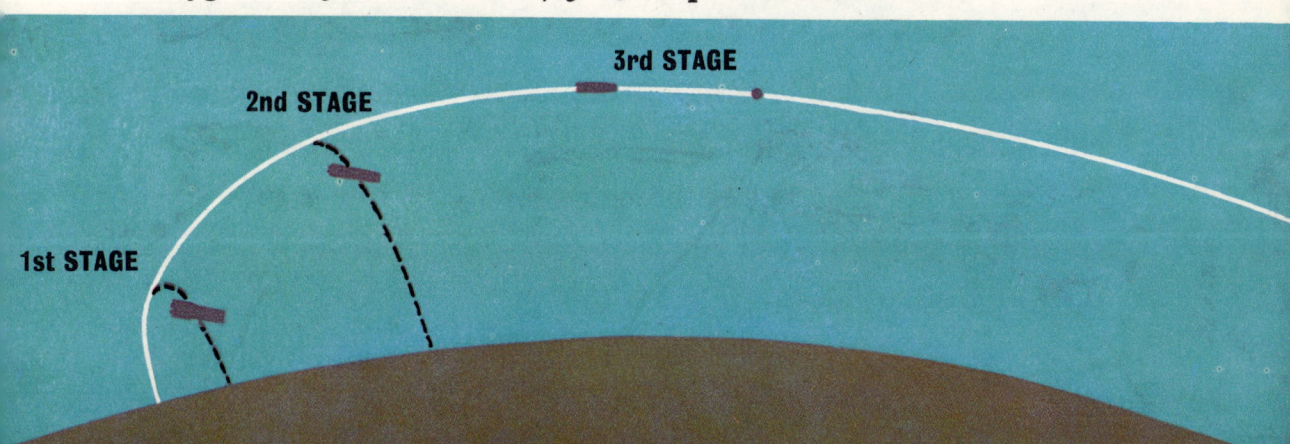

3rd STAGE

2nd STAGE

1st STAGE

We have seen that engines take the energy from fuels such as coal and gasoline and turn this energy into useful work. But how did the energy get into the fuels?

Our nearest star is the Sun which is burning up at the rate of 4 million tons per second and pouring itself out into space in the form of heat, light, X-rays and other forms of *radiation*. A tiny fraction of this falls upon the earth and is used by plants to grow. This has gone on for millions of years. A long time ago, primitive plants, like giant ferns, grew, died and fell into the swamp waters where they grew. Their bodies rotted to form peat which was buried and turned, by heat and pressure, into coal. When we burn coal, we release "bottled" sunshine. Oil, too, is "bottled" sunshine but probably made in another way. Oil is thought to be the substance squeezed out of the bodies of all the tiny sea creatures that have died and sunk to the sea bed over countless centuries.

KEY ■ useful energy
▨ wasted energy

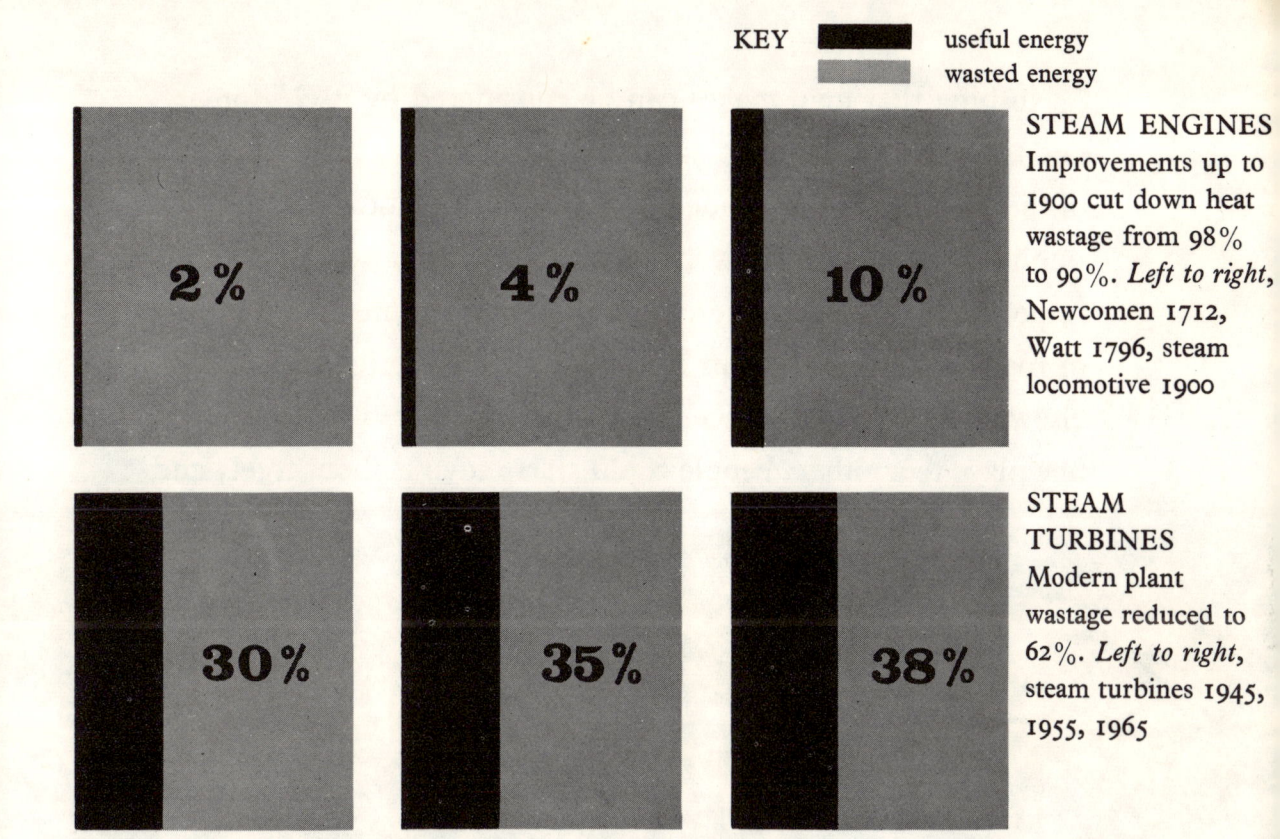

| 2% | 4% | 10% | **STEAM ENGINES** Improvements up to 1900 cut down heat wastage from 98% to 90%. *Left to right*, Newcomen 1712, Watt 1796, steam locomotive 1900 |
| 30% | 35% | 38% | **STEAM TURBINES** Modern plant wastage reduced to 62%. *Left to right*, steam turbines 1945, 1955, 1965 |

Because these fuels are costly and will not last forever, we must use them in such a way that we get the most out of them. We must use them efficiently. The word efficiency, when applied to an engine, indicates how much of the energy which the sun put into these fuels we have been able to use and turn into useful work. But although engines will become more and more efficient, we shall never be able to reach complete efficiency because some energy is always wasted in friction and other processes. For this reason perpetual motion machines can never work.

Nothing that man makes can be considered by itself, for one thing always leads to another. For instance, the invention of the gasoline engine made possible popular motoring and public air transport all over the world, both matters of importance to the common man. The first meant that systems of roads would be built in Europe, North America and elsewhere, which would cut down the time taken to go from one place to another. People could start moving about freely and

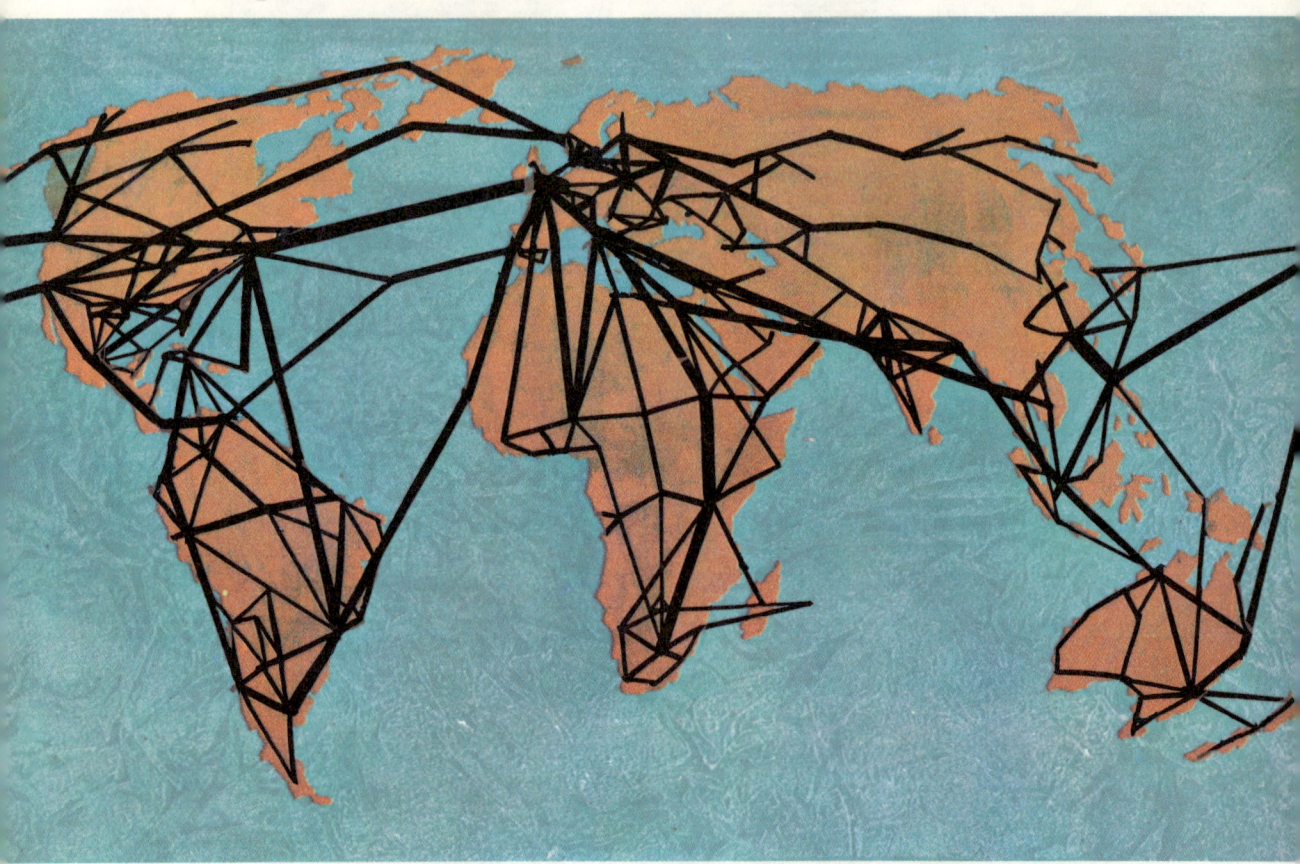

Airlines today link most countries in the world. With jet airliners the furthest place can be reached in a day. The supersonic airliner will circle the earth in 24 hours

getting to know one another over a fairly large area. The big airliners have widened this process and now the fast jet airliners make it possible to get to any place on earth in a matter of a few hours when once it would have taken weeks or months. The growth of the oil industry is another thing that can be traced to the development of the internal combustion engine. At first its main product was gasoline, but now the range of its by-products extends to plastics, fuel oils, detergents and pesticides.

The people who made the first engines in the 18th century could have had no idea that their work was going to lead to all this—and many more developments which are yet to come.

Some of the new words you have read in this book:

By-pass engine. A type of jet in which half the air by-passes the combustion chamber to be mixed with the hot gas at the propelling nozzle.
Capacity (of a cylinder). The volume traced out by the movement of the piston. The capacity of an engine, which is that of all the cylinders added together, roughly indicates the power of the engine.
Combustion chamber. The place in an engine or furnace in which fuel is burned to heat gas, air or water.
Condensation. The process in which vapor (steam) turns into liquid (water).
Crank. A lever arrangement for turning an up-and-down motion into a round-and-round one.
Cylinder. A round iron tube, closed at one end and smooth inside, in which a piston slides up and down.
Double-acting engine. An engine in which the piston is pushed both ways in the cylinders.
Elements. In this case wind, rain, snow, sunshine, etc. (not chemical elements).
Forge. To shape metal (often hot iron or steel) by hammering or squeezing.
Gas turbine. A system in which air is compressed, heated and used to drive a turbine.
Generator. A machine that produces electricity.
Heat exchanger. A device for transferring heat from a hot stream to a cold stream of gas without mixing the two streams.
Helicopter. An aircraft using a rotating wing driven by the engine, so that it can rise from rest straight up into the air without having to run along the ground.
Horizontal. Level with the horizon.
Horse power. The amount of work a horse could do in one minute, that is to raise 150 lbs. of coal 220 ft. in that time.
Internal combustion engine. An engine in which the pressurized gas is made hot by burning fuel in it.
Jet engine (or turbo-jet). A gas turbine in which enough energy is left in the exhaust to form a propulsive jet.
Jet propulsion. Using a jet motor to drive airplanes and rockets forward by internal push.
Locomotive. A machine that can move itself along, usually on wheels and on rails.
Nozzle. A shaped passage that forms a jet from the air or hot gas passing through it.
Oxidant. A gas or liquid mixed with a fuel to make it burn.
Piston. The sliding plug that is pushed in or out of the cylinder.
Propulsion. The act of pushing or driving forward.
Radial engine. An engine whose cylinders are arranged in a circle.
Radiation. Energy (heat or light) that moves through space with nothing to carry it, for instance, the kind of heat that reaches the earth from the sun.
Ram jet. A very simple jet engine having no moving parts.
Rocket. A jet device that carries its fuel and oxidant with it. It can therefore fly in airless space.
Sonic speed. The speed of sound in air. Airplanes experience very high resistance when moving at sonic speed.
Traction engine. A steam-driven road locomotive for pulling heavy loads.
Turbine. A rotating "windmill" machine driven by hot, high-pressure gas and producing power directly in rotary form.
Turbo-prop engine. A gas turbine engine driving an ordinary aircraft propeller.
Thrust. The push produced in an engine by the propulsive jet.
Vacuum. A space from which most of the air or gas has been removed.